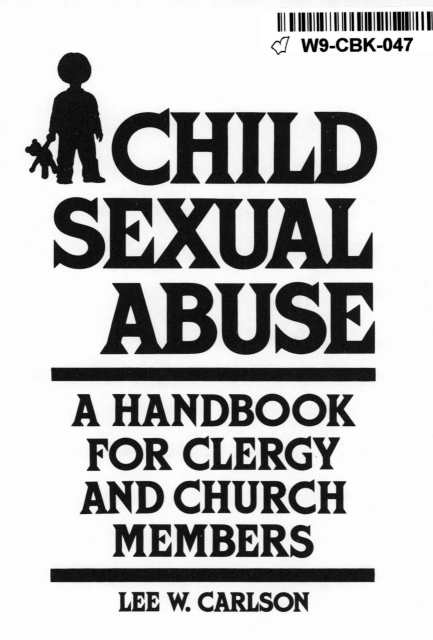

CHILD SEXUAL ABUSE

A HANDBOOK FOR CLERGY AND CHURCH MEMBERS

LEE W. CARLSON

Judson Press® Valley Forge

CHILD SEXUAL ABUSE

Unless otherwise indicated, Bible quotations in this book are from the Revised Standard Version of the Bible copyrighted 1946, 1952 © 1971, 1973 by the Division of Christian Education of the National Council of the Churches of Christ in the U.S.A., and used by permission. Other Bible quotations are taken from the HOLY BIBLE New International Version, copyright © 1978, New York International Bible Society. Used by permission.

LIBRARY OF CONGRESS
Library of Congress Cataloging-in-Publication Data

Carlson, Lee W.
    Child sexual abuse: a handbook for clergy and church members / by
Lee W. Carlson.
        p. cm.
        Bibliography: p.
        ISBN 0-8170-1133-1 : $6.95
        1. Sexually abused children—Pastoral counseling of.   I. Title.
BV4464.3.C37 1988   88-15896
261.8'3—dc19   CIP

The name JUDSON PRESS is registered as a trademark in the U.S. Patent Office.
Printed in the U.S.A.

CHILD SEXUAL ABUSE

for Carolyn,
    who is my life companion
    and my best friend
    and
for Christy, Suzanne, Lynne, and Jenny,
    who bring joy and meaning
    to a father's heart

Acknowledgment

I am profoundly grateful to Ms. Helen Swan for her significant contributions to this book. Helen Swan is a clinical social worker living in Leawood, Kansas. She is the past director of the Johnson County (Kansas) Family Sexual Abuse Center. As a specialist in child sexual abuse, Helen travels widely, lecturing, encouraging, and training professionals. She has produced or coproduced numerous books, articles, and resources on child sexual abuse, including the highly acclaimed film "Bubbylonian Encounter."

In addition to giving much encouragement and advice to me about this subject, Helen has supplied the basic information included in Chapters 2 and 3 of the book.

 Contents

Introduction

Like an iceberg rising sharply in the dark ahead, child sexual abuse is ominously coming to the attention of our society. What we can see is alarming and disturbing, and what we can't see or know, at this time, is menacing and frightening.

Child sexual abuse is any forced sexual contact upon a child who developmentally is not capable of understanding or resisting, and/or who is socially or emotionally dependent upon the offender. Abuse may include fondling, masturbation, genital penetration, or exhibitionism. It is a crime in every state.

The immensity of the problem cannot be overstated. One out of every four girls will be sexually molested before she is eighteen, and one out of every eight or ten boys will likewise experience sexual abuse. These are conservative estimates based on the best available studies and research.

Such sexual exploitation is usually not an isolated fifteen-minute trauma in someone's life; rather, the average incident is a gradual process of abuse spreading over several years, with consequences that stretch over a lifetime. The average age of the child victim is eight.

Nor is it widely understood that sexual molestation within the home is four times more likely to happen than sexual violence from a stranger. Fathers and stepfathers of the victim represent almost half of all sexual offenders. Too often victims grow up to be sexual abusers themselves, thus perpetuating a destructive cycle generation after generation.

My conviction is that, along with other social agencies, the church of Jesus Christ has a critical responsibility in alleviating this life-crippling scar upon humanity. Ministers and priests have a key role to play in any such healing ministry.

There is a need for bringing into the open this blight that Marie Fortune calls "the unmentionable sin."

There is a need for clergypersons to be informed about the problem and to be conversant on appropriate ways of dealing with it.

There is a need for pastors and other church leaders to know how and where to get help from allied helping agencies.

There is a need for the clergy to understand the legal aspects of reporting child sexual abuse incidents to proper authorities.

There is a need to be cognizant of educational resources.

In summary, there is a need for churches to be involved in bringing healing and reconciliation to victims, offenders, and their families. This book is an attempt to meet these needs for clergy and other church leaders. I am convinced that the clergy, when informed and trained, are able to lead their churches in a unique healing ministry.

I am convinced that clergypersons who read this book also care about people. My hope is that with proper understanding, that care can be turned into effective and healing ministry.

This caring and informed approach is demonstrated by the minister in Chapter 1.

1
A Case History

Pastor Ben Chadwick didn't spend a lot of time with the youth of the church, but when he did he listened a lot more than he talked. He made it a point to know what his teenagers were interested in, and each year he braced himself and took the plunge by attending the annual overnight youth "lock-in." Frequently he would encourage individuals to drop by and see him, anytime, for any reason.

Ben was not surprised when thirteen-year-old Maria Hemphill stopped by to see him one day. For some months he had noticed how the normally talkative Maria had grown quiet and withdrawn. Now she seemed nervous as she settled into a chair opposite her pastor. After exchanging some polite remarks, Ben invited Maria to talk.

"Well, Maria, something seems to be on your mind. Care to talk about it?"

With a heavy sigh, Maria cautiously spoke, "Yes, well, you see, my father . . . ah . . . well my father has been doing things . . . to me . . . and it scares me and makes me feel strange."

She paused for a breath, her eyes riveted on her hands, which were clasped tightly in her lap, and continued.

"He makes me do things, that I . . . I don't like."

Pastor Ben, guessing correctly, said, "Are these sexual things that he does with you?"

A quick instant of eye contact accompanied her response, "Yes, yes it is. Oh, Pastor Ben, can you help me?"

Ben had several strong feelings rising within him as the reality of Maria's situation unfolded. There was sadness and pain for Maria's plight; there was anger, almost instantaneous, at Maria's father, who was a former member of the church council and a man highly respected in the congregation and in the community; there was disbelief that such an activity could be going on in this family; and there was more than a moment of internal panic as he pondered *what do I do now?*

In Ben's mind some facts begin to crystallize. He knew that Warner Hemphill was a man uncomfortable with deep feelings and intimate relationships. Ben also knew that such incestuous abuse was far more common than most people imagined. It had not been easy for Maria to share her secret, and so Ben believed that something was definitely wrong in this family and that Maria's story was probably true.

Weighing all these factors, Ben said gently, "I'm glad you told me about this, Maria. Sexual abuse should never be kept secret. I admire your courage in sharing."

Then carefully he continued, "Your father is wrong when he does these acts, and he is definitely in need of help. For his sake . . . and for your own safety, we need to contact Mrs. Robinson at the Social and Rehabilitation Services Office."

Maria's voice trembled with fear, as she pleaded, "Oh, no, no one else must know about this. I thought I could trust you not to tell. If my father ever finds out, I'll be in big trouble." Then as an afterthought she added, "Why did I ever let this happen?"

Ben reassured Maria that she had done nothing wrong, and that her father was fully responsible for the sexual activities. But in order to stop the abuse and to gain help for her father, others would have to know. He admitted that he did not know enough about child sexual abuse to be able to give her all the help she deserved.

"But," he promised, "I will stand beside you and your family, no matter what happens."

Gradually Maria came to agree, and finally she called the child protective services from the pastor's office. Later, when Mrs. Robinson interviewed Maria, along with Officer Simms of the police department, Pastor Ben sat beside her and offered the support of his presence.

Soon Maria was placed temporarily in a foster home. SRS officials investigated the charges and gathered evidence to prosecute Mr. Hemphill, because under the statutes of all states, he had committed a crime.

In the meantime, because he had opted to report this case of incest to the proper authorities, Ben Chadwick came under heavy criticism from Maria's father. Mr. Hemphill verbally accosted his pastor one day in the office of the church. While maintaining his innocence, he threatened to see to it that Ben would be fired. In a rage he threatened legal action and promised revenge for interfering in his family's life.

Although hurting from the fiery attack, Ben refused to be intimidated by the warnings. For one thing, shortly after Maria's visit to him, Ben had explained the sticky situation to two of his most trusted allies in the church, both of whom were on the church council. Ben didn't reveal more than necessary to them, but he did apprise them in general of a delicate problem involving one of the church families.

Warner Hemphill entered into a "diversionary agreement" by which he started psychological treatment. Therapy continued on a weekly basis for eighteen months. During this process he came to feel deep remorse for his deviant behavior, and the family is considering reuniting.

Meanwhile, Maria entered a teenage therapy program that helped her deal with her anger, fear, and guilt. She terminated this group therapy after nine months and is coping well with her high school studies and her life in general. Nevertheless, she still has occasional nightmares and she still questions herself as to why it all happened to her. The nightmares and unanswered questions about her eighteen months of abuse will probably continue to haunt her for the rest of her life.

After the original crisis and turmoil, Pastor Ben lived up to his promise. He maintained close—though sometimes strained—relationships with the victim, the offender, and the family. It was not easy. Sometimes he wished that he had never known. But on his days of clear thinking, he knew he had acted appriopriately and with true pastoral concern.

About six months after the treatment program began, the incest story was shared with the church elders and they became very supportive of the family. This was done, of course, with the permission of all members of the family. Then Maria told her story at a statewide youth conference and later shared it with several youth groups in her hometown. In every case she was affirmed for her openness and thanked for her courage. One result of her sharing was to inspire at least three other girls to report sexual abuse to their pastors.

The cycle of secrecy about child sexual abuse had been broken. The integrity and redemptive ministry of the pastor had been maintained. The possibility of forgiveness and repentance for the offender had been enhanced. Healing had started for Maria and others like her.

This composite case history reveals how a minister or priest might choose to respond in a situation of child sexual abuse. The story has a happy ending (not all do, of course) in order to point out that clergypersons can deal effectively with a complex problem like sexual abuse. In reality situations like this are rarely easy or straightforward. They are likely to be ambiguous and time consuming, with a high risk of alienation possible. Nevertheless, the clergy, when trained and knowledgeable, can perform a vital role in protecting victims, in helping offenders toward accountability, and in alerting congregations to this damaging problem.

The remaining chapters of this book will provide clergypersons with a more detailed understanding of their vital role.

2

The Causes and Signs of Child Sexual Abuse

As leaders in our congregations and synagogues, it is imperative that we be informed about the causes and indications of child sexual molestation. For those who wish for simple explanations and answers, there is likely to be disappointment and frustration. Like most types of child abuse, child sexual abuse is a multifaceted problem with many causes.

There now exist several theories and models of the origins of child sexual abuse. Psychodynamics theories emphasize the psychological traits of the offender. Social learning theorists regard child sexual abuse as behavior learned within a social context (in a past molestation or modeled from a significant adult). Family systems theory would describe child sexual abuse as a symptom indicating other family problems.

An approach by Dr. David Finkelhor proposes a more multidimensional theory that incorporates a number of individual and societal factors. In his book *Child Sexual Abuse*, Dr. Finkelhor describes the four factors that lead to child sexual abuse.

First, there is an individual with a potential to sexually molest a child. This propensity is usually the result of a traumatic childhood or a history of sexual abuse by nonfamily members. For reasons rooted in the individual's childhood, this person has "learned" this abusive behavior, finds sexual abuse emotionally gratifying, or is unable to enjoy sex with appropriate others.

A second factor is that the offender is not able to control his or her desires to molest children. It is suspected that many individuals may have a potential to molest children. However, certain stress factors make it difficult for certain of these individuals to control their behavior. These stress factors may include marital problems, regular contact with children, "life-living" problems, or difficulties with alcohol or other drugs.

A third aspect is that the child is accessible and unprotected. Few children are molested with a protective adult present. Thus, we often see children sexually molested when they are unsupervised by a parent. Even when a protective adult is in the same home, he or she may deny that the abuse happened or feel powerless in making it stop.

Finally, the child does not resist the molestation attempt. Child sexual abuse is a disarming act that leaves many of its victims feeling powerless to protect themselves. Some children may not realize immediately that anything wrong has occurred; other children do have the inner strength and skills to protect themselves from a possible assault. While preventive actions from children can sometimes stop an abusive act, it does not, under any circumstance, mean that a child is at fault if he or she did not exercise protective action. This point will be stressed again in these pages because of the high amount of self-blame that victims place upon themselves.

Physical and Behavioral Indicators of Abuse

While the causes of child sexual abuse are complex and dynamic in nature, it is frequently easy to detect signs of child sexual abuse without fully understanding the underlying problem. These indicators may be classified into three categories: physical signs, psychosomatic complaints, and behavioral indicators.

Physical indicators are those where some physical damage is done to the body. Such signs include the bruising, tearing, or redness of the genitals. Pain in urinating or passing bowel movements may be other telltale signs. A rather obvious indicator is the victim who becomes pregnant especially when it is obvious that a sexual relationship outside the home has not taken place.

Psychosomatic complaints are physical complaints without any known organic origin. This list includes, headaches, stomach aches, back pain, vomiting without cause, and other general stress-related complaints.

The behavioral indicators cover a wide range of situations. A child who initiates inappropriate sexual behavior with peers or who engages in frequent masturbation may be a victim of abuse. School problems, difficulty in sleeping, and eating disorders are behavioral clues to watch for.

Other hints may come in the form of frequent crying or extended periods of depression without expressed reasons. A child may exhibit unusual aggressive behavior or may withdraw into an active fantasy life.

Another somewhat common indicator is the child who does not want to be alone with an uncle, brother, brother-in-law, father, stepfather, or other males.

Some of the indicators listed above may also be caused by other types of emotional problems. However, it must be noted that there are certain behaviors much more common to sexual abuse than to general abuse. This list includes:

1. a child who says he or she has been abused
2. sexually inappropriate behaviors, like grabbing the genitals of others or dressing in sexually provocative clothes
3. using sexually explicit language.

Talking to Suspected Victims

If a child exhibits some or many of the above behaviors, concerned individuals, especially parents, should try to find out what is upsetting the child. Talking directly about this type of problem may be embarrassing and frightening to a child. Therefore, the following five questions may be helpful and less threatening.

- Is anyone doing something that is upsetting to you?
- Is anyone yelling at you or saying things that are hurtful to you?
- Is anyone physically hurting you?
- Is anyone touching you in places he or she shouldn't?
- Is anyone playing secret games with you?

A child who is being molested still may not reveal what is going on, even after gentle questioning. He or she is probably afraid, confused, or feels embarrassed or guilty. Caring adults should continue to be alert and monitor the situation until some reasons can be uncovered for the child's behavior.

Characteristics of Offenders

While there is no general profile of a sexual offender (they come in all sizes, ages, economic backgrounds, and educational levels), there are characteristics that many offenders share in common:

- They have a strong interest in children.
- Offenders may be in youth professions like boy scouts.
- They may be single and uninterested in adult relationships. Sometimes they may be married but spend an inordinate amount of time with a child or with many children.
- Offenders generally have poor self-esteem. While they may appear to be functioning well, they often have a pervading sense of low self-worth. It is not unusual for an offender to appear as a good family man, gainfully employed, and with strong religious convictions.

"Life-living" problems plague many offenders. They tend to have problems in other areas of their life, such as marriage, work, alcohol abuse, drug abuse, aggressive behaviors, or other emotional problems.

They are commonly defensive about their acts. Most sexual offenders have many emotional defenses such as the ability to deny or project onto others the responsibility for the sexual abuse. These defenses are commonly used with other problems in their lives as well.

It is not unusual for an offender to be "king of his castle." Such fathers or stepfathers who sexually abuse their children function in the home as an absolute authority. Their word is law. When Daddy tells his daughter to engage in sexual behavior, she complies. Often such authority is backed up by a strict and rigid religious orientation.

It is rare for a child to tell a clergyperson that he or she has been sexually assaulted. Rarer still is it for an offender to confess such a deed. However, many victims will give clues that they have been molested. Picking up on those signals is critical. I am strongly convinced that members of the clergy do not need to be powerless and ignorant. When clergy recognize the signs of sexual abuse and take appropriate action, as will be discussed in subsequent chapters, they can be a powerful moral force in combatting further molestation and in lessening the long-term emotional damage to children.

3

Understanding the People Involved

A common thought about incestuous behavior sounds like: *How can a father do that to his own daughter? It's unthinkable—repulsive! I can't understand it.*

Sometimes as clergy our sense of moral outrage about child molestation clouds our vision and actually feeds our lack of understanding about the people involved. Popular myths may dominate our thinking. For instance, there is the belief that the greatest danger is from the stranger (usually a seedy, unkempt person). Another erroneous thought is that the majority of offenders are men over fifty. The reality is that by far the greatest danger is from someone the victim knows, and that twice as many offenders are under twenty years of age as are over fifty years of age.

In her book *Sexual Abuse—Let's Talk About It*, Margaret O. Hyde calls for a deeper understanding of child sexual abuse. To that end she asks what you believe about the following statements.

- Sex offenders are usually dirty old men.
- Most child molesters are homosexuals.
- Sex offenders are usually lonely, unmarried men.
- The sexual abuse of children is something new.
- Victims of sexual abuse are weak girls who like it.

- Information about sexual abuse of children increases their chances of being abused.
- If victims of child sexual abuse talk about it, it will make matters worse.

Each of the above statements is false. Some clergypersons would rather cling to the myths than to confront the realities of child molestation. One reason for this is that the reality is often emotionally disturbing and confusing.

Our need is to learn and understand. The following story may help us advance our understanding of the principal actors in the tragedy of abuse.

Annette, age thirteen, spent the night with her best friend Toni. That evening, while no one was in the same room, Toni's father, Mr. Gray, made a pass at Annette and grabbed her breasts. He said that she was very pretty. During the following two weeks Annette was at Toni's house several times. Toni's father again fondled her breasts and said he wanted to spend the night with her.

The following discussion will highlight some of the common feelings and thoughts that different people in the story may experience as a result of the sexually abusive acts. The act of fondling is considered sexually abusive behavior. Sexual abuse is done with the intent of sexually inciting a child or the perpetrator. Touching a child's breasts, even if the child does not resist, is sexual abuse.

Annette: The Victim of the Crime

In this case, one of the initial feelings Annette may have had was confusion—confused feelings about the act and the abuser. Many children have positive relationships with the sexual offender and may even enjoy the adult's attention that is a part of being sexually molested. In many situations, even if Annette experienced the touching as disgusting and unwanted, she may have felt powerless to protect herself. Sexual abuse is a disarming act, one that often leaves child victims responding in a passive, nonprotective manner.

A common feeling that victims of sexual abuse report is fear. Annette may have felt fearful of many different things. She may have been fearful that no one would believe her, that harm may come to Toni's father and/or herself, or that her friend Toni may have been embarrassed. Such initial fears may lead Annette to decide she must endure the abuse, making future reporting even more difficult.

In almost all sexual abuse cases, a child feels some responsibility for the abuse. In the case of Annette, she may have felt that the abuse would not have happened if she had not gone to her friend's house, or had said no to Mr. Gray, or had worn pajamas instead of her nightgown, or had not returned again to the house after the first incident. Such guilt continues to entrap Annette into the abusive cycle and weakens her ability to say no. The continued abuse also lowers the child's self-esteem and leads the child to feel that he or she is a bad person.

Finally, many victims of sexual molestation suffer even more from long-term effects of the abuse. Victims of sexual abuse frequently report profound effects from sexually abusive situations. These effects often plague a victim with serious emotional handicaps in living a happy and productive life.

Mr. Gray: The Offender in the Abuse

While children vary in their responses to sexual molestation, perpetrators of the act do as well. Some sexual offenders exhibit few feelings of remorse, believing that their behaviors were justified and even acceptable. Most sexual offenders, however, experience many of the same painful feelings that the child experiences.

Mr. Gray most likely felt confused about the act. Mr. Gray may have experienced some pleasant sensations such as a sense of intimacy and sexual arousal. At the same time, Mr. Gray most likely felt some guilt and worry that he had emotional problems. He may have been concerned that the act was harmful to the child and that it was morally reprehensible. While he tried to justify that the act was helpful to the child and to himself, usually he was left with some sense that the act was sinful and wrong.

One of the most pronounced feelings that the offender may experience is fear. Mr. Gray most likely was concerned that he would be caught, or that he and his family would suffer social ridicule, or he would be sent to jail, or Mrs. Gray would leave him, or his children would never talk to him again. He may have promised himself that he would never again do such an act, only to feel even more crazy and out of control when he repeated the sexual behavior with another child. His behavior seemed compulsive, leaving him feeling even more powerless over his life and behavior.

Understanding why a person molests a child is always a complex process. In his therapy Mr. Gray would discuss several reasons for his molestation of Annette. These reasons may be based on his childhood experiences as well as his current unfulfilled needs.

There are several different theories that attempt to explain what motivates a sexual offender to molest a child. Again, in understanding Mr. Gray, any of the following three explanations may shed light on his choice to become sexually involved with Annette.

1. *Emotional reasons.* Mr. Gray may have experienced many emotional feelings while he inappropriately touched Annette. Many male offenders report that when they molest a small child they feel "in control," they feel powerful, knowing that the child "will do what they say" and that they will not "reject" the adult. Offenders also report creating a situation similiar to their own past molestation in which they reverse roles and become the aggressor rather than the victim. To an individual who may be feeling powerless, unsuccessful, and unsupported by others, such attention from a child can be a strong reinforcer to continue molestation.

2. *Sexual attraction.* Mr. Gray may have molested Annette because he found Annette sexually arousing, which might be a sexual preference developed in his childhood. Possible

ways a young boy may develop a sexual preference for children may include a past molestation as a child or masturbating while sexually fantasizing about children. Finally, many male offenders admit that their fathers or other significant authority figures molested children, and so these men model what their fathers did, particularly in stressful situations.

3. *Inability to sexually relate with adults.* The molestation of Annette may have occurred because Mr. Gray is not sexually comfortable with adults or does not find them sexually gratifying. His past relationships with his mother or other women may have left him sexually unable to relate to women. A past molestation as a child may have made him feel uncomfortable with adults sexually. Current life problems, such as the inability to relate socially to adults, severe marriage problems, or drug abuse may have limited Mr. Gray's existing sexual contacts. Usually each offender has past and current reasons for molesting a child. Surprisingly, in most situations the offender has genuine concern for the child and values the relationship. None of this is to suggest that the offender's abusive behavior can be justified. It was Mr. Gray who chose to sexualize the relationship with Annette, and he therefore bears full responsibility for the criminal and immoral deed.

Mrs. Gray: The Wife of the Offender

The reactions of a spouse of an offender are often unpredictable. More than likely, Mrs. Gray would not believe Annette's initial report about the abuse. Most women are not aware of their husbands' problems of child molestation. While they may feel that something is wrong with their spouse, they rarely suspect that the problem is child sexual abuse.

Accepting the facts of the abuse will be a painful process for Mrs. Gray. Wives of offenders often feel that they are responsible. They question themselves. *Was I sexual enough with him? Did I miss the problem? Why didn't I stay home that night?*

Women additionally feel embarrassed that they married an offender. Beyond embarrassment there is fear of the social criticism they will receive for having married such an individual, as well as staying with the offender after the report.

Finally, the wife feels a great deal of anger and usually does not know where to direct this anger. Should Mrs. Gray get angry with Mr. Gray, who needs her support? Should her anger be directed at Toni for bringing Annette to the house in the first place? Or should she be angry with Annette for bringing up the matter? It is a good guess that she initially will feel anger toward everyone, only later to wind up blaming herself for being so irrational.

Parents of the Victim

Annette's parents also will have many reactions and feelings to work through. The first reaction that most parents of victims experience is one of disbelief. Could Annette have been mistaken? Was Mr. Gray's intention sexual, or could he just have been having some innocent fun? Could Mr. Gray, the successful family man and engineer, really molest a child? There must be another explanation. Please, let there be another explanation!

When Annette's parents accept the fact that the abuse did occur—and that may take several weeks—their feeling then is anger. When a child is sexually abused, parents generally react and feel strongly. Annette's father may feel like going over and punching out Mr. Gray, or worse may want to murder him. This is a major life trauma for a family. Annette's parents may have the same difficulty as others in not knowing to whom they should direct their anger. Some parents will be angry with the child for going to the house, and most parents feel hurt if their child does not tell them about what happened. It is likely that Annette's parents will also feel responsible for the abuse. Why did they let Annette go to Toni's house? Shouldn't they have been more alert that there was a problem?

This summary and analysis of Annette's victimization is remarkable and instructive for two principle reasons.

First, the participants are all subject to the same basic emotions and reactions. For each person in the tragic drama, there is the possibility of experiencing feelings of confusion, powerlessness, fear, guilt, self-blame, pain, hurt, embarrassment, and anger. For the spouse of the offender and the parents of the victim, there may also be a sense of disbelief.

These are feelings and emotions common to us all, clergy and nonclergy alike. While most of us as clergypersons will not be able to identify directly with sexual abuse behavior, we all have encountered those feelings of confusion, fear, guilt, and so forth. In a sense, that should help our understanding of the feelings of those caught in the throes of child molestation. Our greater understanding in turn enhances our ability to respond caringly and redemptively.

A second learning from all this is that all the participants will need skilled counseling. For the victim and the offender, it will probably be long-term, in-depth therapy. Such therapy is beyond the training and expertise of all but a handful of ministers and priests. We should not deceive ourselves into trying counseling that offers simple solutions or easy forgiveness.

Definitive understanding of how an adult can sexually abuse a child may elude us. Nevertheless, the information of this chapter can help us overcome our initial moral outrage, as well as our informational innocence, and thereby increase the possibility of our being effective ministers to those in dire need.

4

A Theological Perspective—
An Ethical Response

After he had been sexually molested by his baseball coach on an overnight campout, an eleven-year-old boy lamented, "If I had never been born, this never would have happened." Every occurrence of child sexual abuse is a potentially life-shattering event.

Because of the gravity of such episodes, it is incumbent upon us as clergy to grapple with the theological ideas and materials that can inform our thinking and acting. Such inquiry moves us into the biblical record and the sin of abuse, then on into inappropriate reactions and the responses of justice. The purpose of this chapter is to promote an open, healing, reconciling ethical stance for each of us.

The Bible is of little help in terms of offering guidance about the specific matter of child sexual abuse. Not only is the Bible largely silent, but where it does speak, it is insensitive and uncaring toward the victim of sexual violence.

For example, incest surfaces in the story of Tamar, who is raped by her brother, Ammon. As the event unfolds in 2 Samuel 13, Ammon tricks his sister, ignores her protests, and forces her to lay with him. What the biblical record is concerned about in this sinful act is the violation of property rights rather than the violation of personal and civil rights. Women were considered to be property, usually owned by the father or a husband. Ammon's act was an infringement of *the father's* right of ownership. Tamar's reaction of grief and desolation is clearly shown, yet there is no response to her as a victim of personal injustice. This is representative of the manner in which the Bible deals with sexual violence. Each case of rape is handled as a matter of economic injury. This causes Marie Fortune to state, "Much of the distortion about the nature of sexual violence and the treatment of victims is rooted in the Bible."[1]

At the same time the Bible prohibits various forms of incest in passages in Leviticus 18 and 20. The penalty for incest was childlessness (20:21), death (20:11-13), and excommunication (1 Corinthians 5:2,5). The extent to which the Hebrew and later Christian communities of faith carried out these punishments is not certain. Again, what is clear in these texts is the absence of any sensitivity to the plight of the victims of incest.

No passage in Scripture deals with child sexual abuse as such, and maybe this is a happy circumstance when we see how the Bible deals with other acts of sexual violence.

As clergy, our pathway to a more helpful ethical and theological stance is illumined by a review of and perhaps a revision of our understanding of sin. Child sexual abuse is a sin! But what does that mean? What is the nature of the sin in such matters? Who is the sinner?

First and foremost, child sexual abuse is a violation of right relationships. In this sense sin is an alienation, a brokenness, and an estrangement. The estrangement is with God, others, and oneself. Sin is a state of being that is characterized by fractured relationships.

In child sexual abuse the proper, loving, nurturing relationship between adult and child has been undermined, and a broken, destructive relationship is in evidence. So, child and offender are estranged. God and offender also are estranged because God desires loving, caring, nurturing relationships among people. The offender is estranged from his or her own best self. Likewise, the victim may feel separated from God. To the extent that the victim accepts self-blame for what has happened, that victim may feel estranged from inner health and well-being.

When blame and fault for child sexual abuse are being considered, a clear categorical message must be conveyed. The adult perpetrator of abuse is the sinning party. The child is always the victim. While this may be self-evident to some, nevertheless many victims will blame themselves and accept responsibility for what has happened. The eleven-year-old boy who wished he had never been born is an example of such self-accusation. Adults have power over children and may use that power to coerce children into sexual activity. The child never has the power over the adult. Hence, the adult offender is the sinner.

Even so, clergy will sometimes make inappropriate responses to child sexual abuse. Three such improper reactions come to mind.

The first wrong response is for the clergyperson to side with the offender and neglect the victim. A thirty-nine-year-old Midwestern minister had been asked by the mental health center in his community to offer religious counseling to a teenage girl. The young woman had suffered sexual molestation from a highly respected church member, and the incident took place in the church building. Her agonizing questions were, Why did God allow this to happen? How can I ever forgive this man for what he has done to me? Augmenting the trauma of the incident was that some persons in the religious community refused to believe the young woman's story, and were openly supporting the alleged offender. This is not an uncommon situation, particularly where the offender has had a responsible and respectable image in the community.

Members of the clergy should not be guilty of leaping to conclusions about guilt or innocence in a situation of child sexual abuse. But neither should they automatically side with an alleged offender. In between the extremes, the clergyperson should adopt an attitude and viewpoint that will safeguard the one who claims to be victimized.

A second inappropriate response on the part of clergy is to

try to handle it by himself or herself. Some well-meaning clergy may assume that with God's help and with plenty of prayer and faith, the trauma of incest or sexual abuse can be overcome. They are wrong. The complexities and psychological damage of child sexual abuse are so great that a team approach is called for. Social workers, child protection workers, mental health professionals, law enforcement persons, and members of the legal profession are all allies with the clergyperson in resolving abuse situations. Even a highly trained and skilled pastoral counselor must learn to refer situations of abuse to the wider group.

"Do nothing" is a third tempting option for clergypersons. It is less threatening and less of a risk to ignore signs of child sexual abuse. We can justify such nonaction in many ways: "I can't believe such an activity could be going on"; "The man is the head of his household, so who am I to interfere in the affairs of his realm?" "I can't prove that anything wrong is taking place"; "I may jeopardize my effectiveness as a pastor by becoming involved"; "I could lose my job by pushing for justice." All these rationalizations are based either on poor theology or a lack of courage.

There must be a better response to child sexual abuse than any of the aforementioned options. And there is! Marie Fortune suggests that a "response of justice" is needed toward sexual violence. At the heart of such a response is this general principle: As clergy we will always minister to and attempt to protect victims of abuse. The biblical illustrations of such protection of victims are numerous. The New Testament story of the good Samaritan is a striking model of action. Review Luke 10:30-37 to observe the man from Samaria assisting the Jewish man who had been accosted by robbers along the Jericho road.

In her book *Sexual Violence: The Unmentionable Sin*, Marie Fortune breaks down the response of justice into five ethical responses to sexual abuse.

1. *The response of righteous anger*. A hideous crime deserves a passionate reaction. Such anger must find con-

structive release. Jesus experienced this when he cleansed the temple of those who were defiling it.

2. *The response of compassion for the victim.* To cheer up the brokenhearted, to lift up the downtrodden, and to bind the wounds of those who suffer—this is what marks true religion.

3. *The response of advocacy for the victim.* Victims are frequently powerless to seek justice against the offenders and the systems that hurt them. If the clergy refuse such advocacy, who will stand with the victims?

4. *The response of holding the offender accountable for his or her actions.* This involves such issues as admission of guilt, restitution, repentance, understanding, and forgiveness.

5. *The response of prevention.* Now that the issue of child sexual abuse is out in the open, how can the clergy lead the fight to prevent this life-damaging crime?[2]

We have discovered that the biblical material is practically nonexistent, especially where child sexual abuse is concerned. However, principles for action can and must be inferred from a view of sin as estrangement and alienation. Then a solid theological and ethical stance based on justice for the victim can bring healing, forgiveness, and reconciliation.

Yes, it is a gargantuan task! It calls for clergy possessing unusual resolve and superior courage.

5

Discretionary Confidentiality and Reporting Abuse

Rev. John Mellish felt he had no choice. He refused to tell authorities about a confession that he had heard in counseling, in which a man admitted that he had sexually abused a child. Mellish, the pastor of the Margate Church of the Nazarene in Florida, was sentenced to sixty days in jail. However, the Florida law was changed, his sentence was overturned, and he actually spent only one night in jail.

Mellish went to jail over the issue of confidentiality. The dilemma is fairly obvious. Should a clergyperson deviate from the principle of confidentiality in order to protect a child, or should he or she maintain confidentiality and thereby possibly place the child in further jeopardy?

Like all moral dilemmas there are persuasive arguments on both sides. However, I choose not to be neutral. I believe that in general concern for the well-being of potential or actual victims of abuse takes precedence over remaining silent. The shroud of secrecy must be torn. A principle of discretionary confidentiality should be embraced. In point of fact the ethical matter is somewhat different. Seldom does an offender voluntarily confess to a clergyperson, making the Mellish case a rare exception. In talking to numerous ministers and priests, I have discovered few who have heard confessions about child sexual abuse. One trained pastoral counselor, who also pastors a large local church, has had only two such situations come up in over ten years. It is more likely that a child or teenager will come seeking assistance, and that becomes a cry for help from the victim rather than a confession from an offender.

Nevertheless, in this chapter we will examine the idea of confidentiality, reasons for maintaining it, reinforcing the view that protecting victims is the priority, and then reviewing a typical state reporting law.

The purpose of confidentiality is to provide a safe location for a parishioner or client to express concerns, issues, problems, and sins without fear of disclosure. In such a setting it is understood that secrecy will be maintained, and when there is doubt about this, one will hear statements like, "Of course I wouldn't want this told outside this room."

Sissela Bok suggests four practical reasons for confidentiality.

1. An individual's autonomy over personal information.
2. Respect for relationships between persons and for the intimacy that comes with information shared only in a particular relationship.
3. An obligation of allegiance and support.
4. The safety of a place to disclose information which, if undisclosed, would be detrimental to society as a whole.[1]

Obviously, some important values undergird the commitment to confidentiality.

An equally important aspect of confidentiality—in some Christian denominations—is the private and secret confessional experience. For Anglican and Roman Catholic priests, the occasion of confession with a parishioner is sacramental. Whatever information is shared is held in confidence by the seal of confession, with no exceptions. Other Christian communions charge their clergy to maintain all confidences inviolate, even though they do not view confession as sacramental. The Lutheran Church of America, while protecting the confidences of the parishioner, also allows for pastoral discretion in order to prevent a crime.

It becomes evident that a universal rule to fit all ecclesiastical traditions is impossible. In the final analysis it is the clergyperson's own ethical responsibility to decide. For some this will mean absolute secrecy, for others it will mean discretionary sharing of information to protect potential and actual victims of child sexual abuse.

For those not bound by the seal of confession, a careful analysis of the difference between secrecy and confidentiality will be helpful.

Reverend Marie Fortune makes the distinction. "Secrecy is the absolute promise never under any circumstances to share any information which comes to a clergyman; this is the essence of sacramental confession." Such a commitment to secrecy may mean the shielding from disclosure of a murderer, a sexual offender, and so forth. By contrast, confidentiality is less strict and more flexible. "Confidentiality means to hold information in trust and to share it with others only in the interest of the person involved, i.e., with their permission, in order to protect others from harm by them." With confidentiality the clergyperson's own discretionary judgment can be employed to determine situations where persons need protection. Fortune continues, "Confidentiality is not intended to protect abusers from being held accountable for their actions or to keep them from getting the help that they need."[2]

It is this flexible interpretation of confidentiality that I support and recommend to clergypersons.

When a clergyperson struggles to decide whether or not to tell, his or her discretionary judgment is aided by remembering some fairly well-established aspects of criminal behavior. Marie Fortune lists seven such aspects in her previously quoted article.

1. Batterers and incest offenders will do it again unless given specialized treatment.
2. Offenders lie, cover up, minimize, or deny their criminal behavior.
3. Offenders are powerless to help themselves back to nor-

mal relationships and so outside intervention is required.

4. Treatment of offenders is most effective when ordered and monitored by the courts.

5. The cycle of secrecy must be broken before either victim or offender can be helped.

6. The clergy do not have, except in very rare instances, all the therapeutic tools they need to effectively counsel offenders.

7. Quick forgiveness is cheap grace and is unlikely to lead to repentance.[3]

These seven patterns about abusive behavior lend considerable weight to our idea that neither victims nor offenders are helped by strict secrecy. Discretionary confidentiality is the most efficacious way.

Discretionary confidentiality seems better suited to our understanding of biblical ethics. A biblical pattern for helping people who are weak and powerless is clear. The Hebrew people lived out a code of hospitality in regard to widows, orphans, and sojourners. Recall the picture of God in Deuteronomy 10:17-19 (NIV):

> For the Lord your God is God of gods and Lord of lords, the great God, mighty and awesome, who shows no partiality and accepts no bribes. He defends the cause of the fatherless and the widow, and loves the alien, giving him food and clothing. And you are to love those who are aliens, for you yourselves were aliens in Egypt.

It was the responsibility of the community to love and protect the people in their powerlessness.

Another biblical pattern is all about seeking accountability and repentance for those who have offended. Jesus states it clearly in Luke 17:3 (NIV): "If your brother sins, rebuke him, and if he repents, forgive him." A person who sins by harming another, as is the case with child sexual abuse, is to be confronted so that he might seek repentance. Repentance literally means "a change of mind," and sexual offenders need such a change before forgiveness and reconciliation can take place.

These weighty matters—repentance, forgiveness, and reconciliation—should be of primary concern to persons who are clergy.

Now we move to the practical matter of the regulations and procedures for reporting suspected situations of child sexual abuse. The legal requirements for reporting cases vary among our states. Some states that do not require the clergy to report are Washington, California, Kansas, New York, and Ohio. Members of the clergy are encouraged to check their own state law carefully. A copy of such laws is usually available from the juvenile court or the social welfare office.

The Kansas law is typical of states that do not force the clergy to report. It stipulates that doctors, dentists, licensed social workers, nurses, psychologists, teachers, school administrators, and law enforcement personnel when they

> have reason to believe that such a child has had injury or injuries inflicted upon him or her as a result of physical or mental abuse or neglect . . . shall report . . . to the juvenile court . . . or to the department of social and rehabilitation services.[4]

The statute, while not mentioning the clergy, does include "all other persons who have reason to believe . . . may report the matter promptly. . . ." So the clergyperson has the right to report—if not the legal obligation.

The statute later states that physical abuse "includes sexual abuse . . . maltreatment or exploiting a child to such an extent that the child's health, morals, or emotional well-being is endangered." It also defines "child" as someone under age eighteen.[5]

According to Kansas procedures the process of reporting is straightforward. The report is made first to the social welfare office, and if that office is closed, then to law enforcement officials. The report may be made orally by telephone and then followed by a written report if requested. Such reports shall contain the names and addresses of the child, his or her parents or guardians, the child's age, the nature and extent of the injuries, and other evidence that might be helpful in establishing either the cause of the injury or the identity of the person alledged to be responsible.[6]

Anyone reporting a suspected act of child sexual abuse is immune from any liability, civil or criminal, which might be incurred or imposed. Such immunity from prosecution should be an encouragement to the clergy and others to help stem the tide of child sexual abuse.

To reiterate an earlier point, clergypersons are urged to find out for themselves the exact nature of the state laws regarding reporting of abuse. Ignorance of these laws is irresponsible.

In closing, Seth Dawson offers a succinct summary of the issue of confidentiality.

> The premises supporting confidentiality are strong, but they cannot support practices of secrecy—whether by individuals, clients, institutions, or professionals—that undermine and contradict the very respect for persons and for human bonds that confidentiality was meant to protect.[7]

6

After Reporting, Then What?

There is a recurring question/concern that arises when members of the clergy discuss the reporting of suspected child sexual abuse. It is often phrased in this fashion: What safeguards are there to protect those who may be falsely accused? The question may be followed by the recitation of a story about someone whose reputation has been ruined either by false accusations or by irresponsible and shoddy investigating procedures. Such a concern for justice is commendable, because "innocent" adults have suffered. However, the question may reveal something of the inadequate and/or misleading information that some ministers and priests possess. It seems important for the clergy to be in the know when it comes to understanding child abuse investigative processes.

In this chapter we will review the processes of investigation and the procedures of the legal system in attempting to deal with sexual offenders.

Let's follow Maria Hemphill through the various systems with which she came in contact. Maria is the thirteen year old who confided in her pastor about her history of incest. While her story is a composite of many such incidents, it is nevertheless an accurate portrayal of reality for thousands of young women.

At her pastor's insistence Maria met with Social Worker Barbara Robinson and Police Detective Robert Simms. Because of the trusting relationship between Pastor Chadwick and Maria, he was allowed to sit in on the first interview. The inclusion of a pastor in such an interview is rare, but it was something that helped Maria feel more comfortable.

Meeting in an unused classroom at school, the social worker and the detective began a series of questions to ascertain the precise facts surrounding Maria's abuse. Mrs. Robinson asked Maria to tell her story and they listened and took notes, occasionally interjecting questions for clarification. The session was recorded on a tape recorder. (For children under thirteen there may be a videotape of the interview, which is now admissible as evidence in the courts of most states).

Mrs. Robinson, who had conducted many such interviews, pressed ahead gently but firmly to discover the specifics of the situation. On what date had the last incident occurred? Where did it happen? What specific sexual act took place? How frequently have such acts taken place?

Because a criminal act had taken place, Detective Simms was present to represent governmental authority. He, too, had experienced several previous interviews and had learned to be a caring and gentle investigator.

Once her silence about her secret was broken, Maria was eager to share her story and sensed relief that the interview was handled in such a gentle and casual manner.

The whole purpose of this interview was to gather evidence for a criminal prosecution. Hence, the more specific the information the better it was in terms of preparing a legal case. The first interview (after reporting) was the crucial one, because Maria would normally have better recall of the details of what actually happened.

Following this initial interview, Mrs. Robinson took immediate steps to remove Maria from her home and put her in the protective custody of a foster family.

Maria's parents, Warner and Sally Hemphill, registered various reactions to the news of what was happening. Detective Simms interviewed Mr. Hemphill about the alledged incest, making him aware of the nature of the accusations. Warner protested angrily about removing Maria. He maintained his innocence, playing the part of a stern disciplinarian, which he was. Sally, a quiet, taciturn woman in her forties, was surprised and at first disbelieving.

Later, Robert Simms presented the written report and the audiotape to County Attorney Max Travers. The young county attorney went throught a careful ritual of examining the evidence, as he had done with numerous similar reports. Concluding that there was sufficient evidence to proceed, he immediately secured an arrest warrant for Warner Hemphill.

Police Detective Simms arrested Mr. Hemphill three days after Maria was taken from the home. He was charged with three counts of incest and informed of his rights at a first court appearance. Bond was set by the judge, and Warner Hemphill, with adequate financial resources, was able to post the bond money and was released that same day. His preliminary hearing, during which time the judge would determine whether there was probable cause that a crime had been committed by Mr. Hemphill, was scheduled to occur in three weeks.

Meanwhile, Barbara Robinson had visited with Sally Hemphill two times, trying to help Maria's mother accept reality. Gradually, Sally's disbelief receded and a small tidal wave of fury washed through her. How could Warner do such a thing? Her anger toward her husband was deep and yet controlled. Surprisingly, she began to question herself and ultimately to blame herself. "I should have been more alert," she lamented to Mrs. Robinson. Within a week the social worker had arranged with the community mental health center to provide ongoing therapy for Mrs. Hemphill.

In the reconstruction of this family, now torn asunder by incest, Mrs. Hemphill would later become a key builder.

After his bond release Warner Hemphill rode a roller coaster of emotions. One day he stormed into Pastor Ben's office, angrily charging him with meddling in "my family," and threatening to have the pastor fired. The next day, in a more rational mood, he recognized the futility of his attack. He began to struggle with his conscience. He wrestled with his private fears about what people would think of him, and the dark cloud of imprisonment that hung over him. Occasionally he thought about Maria because he missed having her around. Rarely did he think about how he had hurt her. Out of such a mix of feelings, Warner Hemphill made a decision.

Maria sometimes wondered if she had made the right choice in disclosing her problem. So many consequences stemmed from that choice, not the least of which was that she now was separated from her family. Her foster parents were understanding people, but still it was no substitute for the real thing. She missed her mother. She missed her own room. She even missed her father.

Several weeks after Maria's first interview, a second interrogation took place. The parties represented were officials from the welfare office, the police department, and the county attorney's staff. Her father's lawyer was also present. Again she told her story, and somehow it was harder this time. First off, she didn't want to tell it again, but she had to. Her memory was not as sharp about details, times, places, and so forth. The lawyer asked questions, and while he was polite, there was a hard edge to his questioning, as if he really were saying, "Come on now, all this really didn't happen."

Maria felt very tense and uncomfortable.

He had seen it happen before, and so County Attorney Travers was not surprised when Warner Hemphill, through his attorney, admitted his guilt, and asked for a diversionary agreement. With no prior felony convictions, and with his admission of guilt, Warner seemed like a good candidate for the diversion program. The community mental health psychologist conducted an evaluative interview with Mr. Hemphill, determining finally that he did seem able to benefit from such a program.

A document was drawn up, stipulating the requirements of the agreement. In general it stated that in exchange for the dropping of criminal charges, the defendant agreed to enter into an extended period of regular therapy. If and when the defendant failed to continue in therapy, the county attorney could proceed with prosecution in the case. This kind of "incentive" is usually needed to get men like Mr. Hemphill into treatment. All members of the Hemphill family agreed to the diversion program as well.

The goal of the diversion program was the reuniting of the Hemphill family for harmonious living free from sexual or other abuse. The fulfillment of such a goal would normally take at least two years.

Throughout this complicated and lengthy period of legal procedures and agreements, Pastor Ben Chadwick maintained a high level of visibility and involvement. In his role as pastor, attempting to minister to the whole family, Rev. Chadwick mostly steered clear of the systemic processes described in this chapter and concentrated on being a supportive, caring, spiritual presence to all. It was not easy! But he was sustained by his conviction that repentance, forgiveness, healing, and reconciliation are at the heart of pastoral ministry. The most, and the best, that he could do would be to help the Hemphill family wrestle with such issues.

Investigative, organizational, and legal procedures are not uniform across the nation. The processes detailed above are somewhat typical of Lyon County, Kansas, and of many other counties that have created a cooperative approach to child sexual abuse. However, probably a majority of political subdivisions across the country are not as advanced. They function with no mental health center, no welfare office, or no legal services that are readily available. In some legal jurisdictions county attorneys and/or district judges are unenlightened or misinformed about the complexities of child sexual molestation.

It cannot be stressed too often or too strongly that we ministers must become informed about the helping systems in our communities. We must learn through our own initiative and exploration how those systems operate.

An enlightened clergy—this is the path of responsible pastoral ministry!

7
Toward Healing for All

Maria Hemphill felt nervous and ill at ease. This was her first group therapy session, with six other girls present, and the safest course seemed to be to keep quiet and listen. She noticed that there was a lot of friendly, playful interchange among the girls. They kidded one another about boyfriends and they genuinely seemed to care about one another. As matters became more serious, Maria was surprised at how well everyone paid attention to the person speaking. They were attentive listeners. She was impressed.

After some introductions and an icebreaker question that everyone answered, Susan, a tall girl about Maria's age, was invited by Mrs. Breman to tell her story.

"I was about nine when my father first came to me. Mother was gone that night playing cards with her friends. When he came to tuck me in, I asked him a question about sex. Instead of telling me, he showed me his penis. That was the first time. Another time he asked me to touch it, and I was so afraid and confused that I did. I felt strange and uncomfortable, but I couldn't say no."

"Why didn't you tell your mother?" Sarah asked.

Susan responded in a soft voice, "I was afraid she wouldn't believe me." Maria was amazed at how honest Susan was and how everyone seemed to want to help her. In another way it was an eye opener for Maria, too. She was not alone in suffering the fear and confusion that went along with those uninvited midnight touches. She thought to herself that maybe this might not be such a bad group after all!

In this chapter we are dealing primarily with healing for all persons who are involved in child sexual abuse. As ministers we all believe in and support healing. Jesus was a healer, and so were various other biblical leaders.

Healing is the hoped-for end result of a large portion of our pastoral work.

In matters of child sexual abuse, healing must be envisioned in comprehensive terms. This means that our task as ministers is to support a holistic practice of healing that includes both psychological well-being and spiritual health.

For the family enmeshed in sexual molestation, therapy and theology form the divided yet parallel roadway toward healing. This chapter will describe the processes and aims of various treatment programs and also chart the major road markers toward spiritual healing.

The ultimate goal of treatment programs is rebuilding a family that is free from sexual abuse. Programs are for victims, for families, and for offenders. Such treatment interventions were largely unheard of just ten years ago. Consequently, there is a general sentiment among therapists that we are still learning about the procedures that work best.

These same authorities agree that professional therapy is absolutely essential for those caught up in sexual abuse, especially where there is long-term incest involved. David B. Peters speaks for many: "It is my professional opinion that all incest cases . . . require professional intervention."[1] Peters, coming from a Christian framework, has worked in California as a counselor with sexual abuse cases since 1968. The quality of that intervention is questionable unless the therapist has had special training in the complexities of child sexual abuse. The emotional scars left by incest will not be healed by self-taught practitioners, whether they be purveyors of mental health or religion.

An overview of these treatment programs will help us as clergy to be more supportive of psychological efforts toward healing.

For Victims

Victims like Maria have a plethora of emotional and educational issues to work through. The first issue is the establishment of blame. The tendency for victims to blame themselves is powerfully strong. "I could have done better," they will say. Or, "Why did I ask?" "I should have been more careful." To place the burden of blame and guilt where it belongs (on the offender), is crucial, difficult and usually repetitive work. In group therapy, which is the primary and preferred mode of treatment for victims, Maria's friends become cotherapists in reminding one another that blame belongs with the offender.

Ambivalent feelings toward parents is a second emotional issue. Children and youth are almost always angry about what has happened. Commonly, they have more intense anger toward their mother than toward the offending father, brother, or uncle. "Mother should have known," or "She should have protected me," victims will bitterly complain. At the other extreme, even though she detests his actions, Maria also misses her father. She loves him still because he has supplied the vast majority of attention and support that she has received at home. Even perverse sexual activities can have nurturing aspects to them.

Other feelings that confound victims are fear and confusion. The fear of being victimized again is prevalent, as are fears about what the future will bring. Some girls have superstitious fears of ghosts and horror movies that detract from their emotional strength and coping powers. Teenage victims frequently experience fearsome nightmares that are usually a reenactment of abusive experiences.

Maria's group therapist, Mrs. Breman, is constantly encouraging her girls to verbalize their anger, fears, and their nightmares. Only as these matters are openly expressed within an atmosphere of trust and support will their power be dissipated and the power of healing begin.

Parenthetically, let me say that I have not the slightest doubt that God is involved in such healing. This is true whether the therapist is a professing Christian or not. Biblical examples of God using secular systems and persons to bring about repentance and spiritual health are ample.

A fourth cluster of emotional and relational issues centers in trust, intimacy, and self-esteem. Victims who have been sexually abused, especially by a friend or relative, suffer a loss of confidence and trust in people that may persist for many years. They reason to themselves, with some justification, that if they have been betrayed by their own fathers, how can they ever really have faith in anyone? "All men are like this" is the next logical and devastating conclusion. When abuse has continued for months or even years, young women and men come to equate intimacy in human relationships only with sexual activity. The damage that all this does to one's sense of self-worth is all too obvious. Self-esteem is crushed. Without therapy, victims are doomed to be wounded souls, perhaps for life.

In her attempt to bring healing to her group, Mrs. Breman sometimes becomes a teacher, employing specific educational material. She teaches sex education because the girls typically are confused and misinformed about human sexuality. She promotes assertiveness training because the girls must learn to defend and protect themselves. She builds communication skills because the girls are accustomed to secrecy, distrust, and repression of emotions. She teaches about family systems because the girls often are caught in role reversals, acting as a mother to younger siblings or as a mistress to a father or stepfather.

She is attempting to help Maria and her friends to move from being victims toward becoming survivors. It is an arduous task. The average length of time in therapy is one year. Maria makes faster progress so that after only nine months her group treatment ends.

One of the initial objectives of healing, unmentioned until

now, is the establishment of the mother-daughter bond. This effort usually runs concurrently with group therapy. The bonding process is a two-way responsibility whereby the mother admits her complicity, ignorance, or denial, and the daughter shares her anger, outrage, and betrayal. The desired result is to trust and rely upon each other again (or for the first time). The bonding process is started just as soon as possible after the discovery of abuse. Peters says,

> If the mother-daughter bond can be established, a very important step has been taken in the healing of both the victim and her family. If not, treatment will be an uphill battle and the chances of saving the family intact will be greatly reduced.[2]

Sally and Maria Hemphill met with Mrs. Breman five times in the days and months following the discovery of abuse. At the second meeting Maria unloaded years of pent-up hostility and anger on her mother, who Maria often had felt was emotionally distant and cool. Sally cried, tearfully defending herself and yet pleading for understanding. It was a painful exchange and yet it was a time of reality and truth, probably the best they had ever shared. The bonding had begun.

For Families

Treatment programs for the nonoffending parent (usually the mother) are commonly of lower priority than therapy for victims. Such programs are generally less sophisticated and more experimental than those for victims. Nevertheless, where such therapy is in place, families have greater hope and a better opportunity for reunification.

Sally Hemphill benefitted in several ways through her several months of counseling. She first was helped to accept rather than deny the reality of child sexual abuse in her home. Joint counseling and confrontation with Maria moved Sally to rethink, for the first time, her own sense of abject and near-total dependency on her husband. Family roles were redefined so that Sally began to reassume her role as mother. Such a transition was not easy for her, nor for Maria, who resisted giving up the power and control she had inherited by default. It was an issue they would continue to encounter for several years beyond therapy.

At the end of her personal therapy, Sally was encouraged to enroll in an assertiveness training class, and for ten weeks she met with other women, many of whom were victims of wife battering. Gradually—painfully—Sally began to learn how to speak for herself and how and when to stand up to Warner.

One tipoff of her progress was in her self-perception. A year after the revelation of child sexual abuse, Sally liked herself more than she ever had in her life.

Such success in treating the mothers of victims is still somewhat rare for several reasons. Programs like this have lower priority, and due to their spasmodic implementation are less tested. Then, too, there are no external controls on mothers. It is a voluntary activity rather than one mandated by the court, as is the situation for offenders.

For Offenders

There are two types of programs for offenders, one of which, the diversionary agreement, was mentioned earlier. The other offender program advocates punishment for the offender as a part of treatment. Punishment in this sense usually means conviction of the offender on charges of sexual abuse, subsequent imprisonment, and/or probation while therapy is continuing. Both styles have their supporters among child protection workers, and neither has any clear-cut superiority over the other. The important factor here is that therapy is essential for offenders if they are to be allowed to rejoin their families.

It is useful to know the distinction between the two classes of child sexual abuse offenders. First, a pedophile is a molester who has a strong, almost exclusive preference for children in sexual relationships. The pedophile is a predatory individual who carefully plans his crimes. He usually selects children he doesn't know to attack. True pedophiles represent a small minority of offenders and respond poorly to all forms of treatment programs.

Regressed molesters are those who usually confine their activity to their own family or to other people they know. Warner Hemphill is a regressed offender who, like many such molesters, himself was a victim of sexual abuse as a child. For him the molestation started as an impulsive, unplanned episode with Maria. Before detection it had grown into such a strong compulsive behavior that he was almost powerless to counteract it, even as an alcoholic often has great difficulty in ending destructive drinking. Time and again in the early months of abuse, Warner promised himself that he would never again go to Maria. His guilt was great, but the pleasure he derived through the abuse was even greater. As a result, like the vast majority of offenders, he yielded to his compulsion and continued his victimization of Maria.

The purpose of group therapy for Warner was to help him overcome his obsession and to reeducate him to live out responsible adult sexual roles. Toward that end therapist Duane Elston worked to help Warner and the others with the following issues.

1. To accept full responsibility for their abusive behavior.
2. To identify and banish the malignant influence of Warner's abuse as a child.
3. To learn a pattern of socialization based on empathy and equality rather than coercion and male superiority.

One day in group therapy Warner was making excuses for his abuse of Maria. "She never protested or said she didn't want me to do it," he rationalized. Suddenly he was cut short by Joe, a veteran in the group.

"Cut the crap, Hemphill. You know she was scared to resist you. Besides, admit it . . . you were turned on . . . it was fun."

Warner made a mild retort, but soon fell silent. In his private pondering he knew Joe had spoken the truth. It would take several more months of counseling before Warner could admit it aloud to the group. When he did, it was a giant stride toward accepting full responsibility for his crime.

The resocialization of Maria's father was a slow, step-by-step struggle that consumed eighteen months of weekly therapy sessions. One phase of the therapy was a face-to-face meeting with Maria in which he made a confession and asked for her forgiveness. Eventually Warner returned home, first on a trial basis, and then for good. Even so, the child protection team remained in close contact with both Sally and Maria Hemphill because the likelihood of a recurrence of abuse remained fairly high.

Spiritual Health

While some professionals do not take seriously the value of spiritual concerns, members of the clergy cannot ignore them. We must attempt what we were called to do—and what we do best—and that is facilitating God's healing in people's lives. We are spiritual health mentors, or at least that is a worthy goal for our ministry.

Spiritual healing in circumstances of child sexual abuse pours the oil of repentance and forgiveness on the wounds of anger, guilt, self-degradation, and hatred. The hoped-for and desired result of our tender and firm ministry is reconciliation. Family members are reconciled to one another and estranged individuals are reconciled to our Creator God.

Let's look briefly at each of the three cardinal theological realities: repentance, forgiveness, and reconciliation.

The issue of repentance pertains to the offender. Repentance is predicated upon a confession of wrongdoing. When Warner Hemphill admitted to himself and his group the harm he had done to Maria, he took an invaluable step toward his ultimate healing. Later, he made the same confession of wrongdoing to his pastor. Ben Chadwick heard that admission of sin and guilt, knowing that confession, though necessary, was not enough. Over a period of several weeks, they talked about repentance. Pastor Ben explained that repentance meant "a change of mind" that led to new and different behavior. Repentance for Warner Hemphill signified a turning from abusive sexual acts to a caring but nonsexual relationship with

Maria. Warner's act of repentance was sincere but he continued to struggle with his compulsion for many months, such was its power over him.

Now to repeat an earlier warning. Far too often offenders suddenly become "religious" in order to avoid either jail or treatment. Those of us in a helping profession like the ministry are particularly vulnerable to manipulative offenders, so we must maintain a healthy skepticism about confessions and repentance. "Cheap grace," as Bonhoeffer called it, benefits no one and here often leads to further victimization of children.

Equally difficult is the issue of forgiveness by the victim. Some therapists do not concern themselves with forgiveness, but as ministers who are concerned about the spirit and soul of persons we cannot avoid it. Being commanded to forgive, as we are in the Bible, actually does little to facilitate the process because forgiveness seems to be more than an act of willpower. Forgiveness toward a sister or brother is an act of the Spirit. It is not well understood by Christians and probably even less practiced.

According to Marie Fortune,

> In order to be authentic, forgiveness must be based on the following:
> —a conscious choice on the part of the victim to let go of that experience of pain and anger
> —empowerment of the victim through God's grace
> —an experience of justice by the victim.[3]

The choice to let go of anger cannot be rushed, and time may be the only healing power that enables a victim to choose to forgive. Without God's grace, as known through prayer and divine presence, forgiveness seems impossible. The justice required is some concrete expression of repulsion and/or sadness about the wrongdoing. This usually is the confession and repentance by the offender.

Can young children forgive in this way? My first impulse is to say no. Younger children ages five, six, and seven cannot understand such a deep theological issue. My more reflective judgment (and guess) is yes. On a very simple level, children let go of anger and move on with an elemental trust in God. I am not saying that later adult therapy will not be needed, because the psychic scars will remain. Nevertheless, children do move on, and some at least are reconciled to their once abusive fathers.

As pastors our distinctive gift is to offer families and especially victims the resources of God. As Cooper Wiggen puts it

> As the victim adjusts and heals, a psychological or spiritual scar tissue may develop. At some point in our confessional experience, I offer her (the victim) the opportunity to ask God into her scar tissue. She can make a decision to expose her trauma to God in hope that God will actually affect her health.[4]

Reconciliation is the ultimate result of repentance and forgiveness. It is a blending of the two and the outcome is a coming home of two estranged parties. In child sexual abuse situations, reconciliation looks like a literal coming home and thus a new beginning for the family.

Such a reunion and starting over is never to be confused with some ideal, sinless state, any more than our personal reconciliation to God means perfection in this life.

For the Hemphill family reconciliation only came after many prior conditions had been fulfilled. Treatment programs for Warner, Sally, and Maria were essential. Another important condition was the empowerment of Sally to be a strong woman and mother. Warner's repentance was an invaluable link in the chain of healing. Forgiveness by Maria, though painful and long in coming, enabled a new beginning for the Hemphills.

Perhaps the illustration of Maria and her family is too idealized. We can be assured that in cases of child sexual abuse the process often may not reach the stage of reconciliation. Yet where is progress made on entrenched evil, if there is not an ideal to reach for? From my faith perspective I maintain that all things are possible with God, even the rehabilitation of a child molester, even the forgiveness and healing of a victim, even the reconciliation of a family. Healing is possible!

As ministers we can be partners if we choose a comprehensive system of healing. In that partnership we have a unique, must we not fearfully admit, *indispensable* role to play. "We are needed by those who suffer," says Cooper Wiggen. "Their voices and their wounds are a word of God for us all."[5] Our role is to encourage victims and offenders and families to invite God into the scar tissue of their lives!

8

Awakening the Sleeping Giant

Most congregations are either uninformed or unaware or both when it comes to the gravity and extent of child sexual abuse in our society. "A sleeping giant" is the image that may best portray the church's potential for involvement.

By way of rousing the giant—that's you and me—let's consider the true account of one mother as her church sought to minister to her family while they recovered from the trauma of incest.

* * *

Becoming a single parent after thirteen years of marriage was a shock to my system, but it was mild compared to our family's encounter with sexual molestation for the following year.

My first awareness that something could be wrong came when my daughters began reacting strangely to their weekend visits to their father's home in another city. From the toddler to the young teenager, each of the three became increasingly upset and reluctant, but they had trouble talking about the reasons why. I felt inadequate to deal with their concerns and made arrangements to have them start seeing a competent child therapist. A few months later, I was called in to meet with the oldest child's counselor after her therapy session. I could not have guessed what would follow.

"Joan, sit down," Elinor began, "and try to listen carefully. Melissa has just told me that Neil sexually molested her during the last weekend visit. It seems that it may have happened before, too, at least once. Also, before her session today, Neil called me and admitted that he had been molesting her. They're both pretty upset right now. . . ."

I heard the rest of what the therapist said through a thick fog. She would have to report to the authorities; Melissa needed a lot of support and comfort from me; and I needed to have someone stay with me that night since Neil sounded desperate and angry on the phone.

I turned to my church, both laypersons and clergy, in the weeks to come. My first contact with my church family after the crisis broke came immediately. On the night I was informed of the situation, my family needed to eat dinner, and Melissa and I both were too upset to even think about cooking. I phoned Phyllis, a Stephen Ministry lay caregiver, who had been visiting with me weekly. All I could manage to tell her was that something was very wrong and that we needed some dinner. She asked no questions but promised to pray, and in two hours a hot meal was delivered to our door. We talked often in the next few months, Phyllis and I, and she mostly listened and let me know she cared. She didn't pretend to understand everything I was going through, but we cried together a lot. Phyllis never doubted mine or the children's words about what was happening, and she never told anyone about our conversations, either. Looking back, I realize how essential her helping qualities of acceptance, support, and confidentiality were, and how rare.

During that first week I also contacted my pastor. In our conversations my pastor's response to our family's situation varied greatly. Initially I had to take a month off work to manage court appearances and to deal with the girls' being upset and fearful around the clock. My pastor conceded that this leave was necessary but went on to chide me for not finishing several projects in progress. He remarked that appearing responsible was very important for future job prospects. I was hurt and puzzled by his remark because I certainly had not chosen to have a child of mine be a victim of violent crime. Later, he offered to have the church pay the two older girls' fees in full for the coming church summer camp. By contrast, this was a real and practical help to all of us.

During the next few months, with Melissa's permission, we let more people know what had happened. Some responded with a kind hug and offers of help, but they also seemed stunned and bewildered. More often, to my surprise, people questioned whether Melissa or I were inventing this story out of spite or some other motive. Others admonished us to forgive and forget and not make too much of the situation. It gradually became clear to me that few people in our church family understood the gravity of the long-term trauma of child sexual abuse. Even hearing about it was painfully awkward for them.

One encounter raised my hopes considerably about six months after the first reporting of the abuse. The time came for me, as an intern, to be interviewed by our church's staff relations committee. The committee asked if there was any way the church could minister to my family. I replied that if three families would become involved with my children, each taking one of the girls on occasional outings or including them in a simple family day, it would lessen the stress on all of us and alleviate our feelings of isolation. The committee agreed and promised to get to work on that request. Sadly, the plan never materialized. We never heard anything else about it.[1]

* * *

The help rendered by the church in this story is both encouraging and sad. My guess is that it is all too typical. While some members are thoughtful and sensitive, most are stunned, bewildered, and inept in responding with Christ's love. How can the giant awaken from its slumber?

The rest of this chapter will focus on ways that the local church can be alerted. The giant, when awake and clear-eyed, can render invaluable service for the sake of victims, offenders, and their families.

For Parents

If innocent children are to be protected from the menace of child sexual abuse, parents are the key. First and foremost I am speaking to parents within the church family. Effective parent training is essential in order to break the vicious cycle of child molestation within the home. When parents are alert and united in their resolve, then *their* children are safe. This is especially true when combatting incest. Father-daughter incest—which is the most prevalent situation—is almost always carried on in secrecy.

So what can parents do? Dr. Peter Coleman, coordinator of Child Protective Services in Tacoma, Washington, offers a basic strategy which, if practiced, would help protect children from sexual abuse. Dr. Coleman advises mothers and fathers (both) to gather the whole family together "and tell your daughters and sons, no matter what age, two years on up, one year on up, if *anyone* touches your penis, your vagina, your buttocks, your breasts, let's talk about it. When mother and father do that together, there are no secrets."[2]

Obviously Dr. Coleman is right. Such an understanding within the family circle will go a long way toward breaking the conspiracy of silence that shrouds sexual abuse. Every family in the church with children can be encouraged and taught to do what Dr. Coleman suggests.

Such teaching might well take place in specially designed parent training sessions devoted to protecting children from sexual abuse. Such sessions for parents would focus on healthy sex education for children and would assist parents in teaching their children that sexuality is a beautiful gift from God to be used in appropriate fashion. Included in such a positive orientation would be advice and guidance about sexual abuse. The sexual abuse content of such training would deal with offenders, the causes and effects of abuse, and prevention of molestation and incest.

Parent training should be done periodically with the blessing and participation of the pastor. Liberal use of community leadership is recommended and needed. People with expertise in dealing with child sexual abuse abound in larger communities and are often most willing to share their knowledge with churches. They simply need to be asked. In smaller communities where resource persons are scarce or nonexistent, the task for churches to provide such parent training is complicated. But the situation is not hopeless. Parents can go to workshops in other cities that have been scouted out and recommended by their church. Or one pastor in the small community can be designated to receive training that he or she would then share with all the churches and parents in town. Of course, sometimes leaders can be brought in from out of town to provide needed sessions. It goes without saying that the pastor's role in all this is to be a supporter, an encourager, a planner, and most importantly, a learner himself or herself.

When parents are better sex educators and are better informed and more understanding of child molestation, at least one eye of the giant is open!

For the Children

Churches should do everything within their power to protect children from the ravages of sexual abuse. One excellent way to do this is to boost public school programs that address the issue of child sexual abuse. While some school systems have proven to be unworthy of trust or are hesitant in acting to prevent abuse (which is the case in my hometown), the majority would welcome the opportunity to be allies with the church.

In truth such cooperation is mostly uncharted territory. When the church takes the initiative in such endeavors with the school, it is an unmistakable sign to the community that the church cares and really means business. Not a bad reputation to have, is it?

Among the scores of prevention programs that are available, let me mention two that merit consideration. Both deal with the "good touch/bad touch" facet of prevention.

"Bubbylonian Encounter" is a play, a film, and a videotape produced in 1980 by the Kansas Committee for the Prevention of Child Abuse. Helen Swan, a co-author of the production, lists the following goals for this resource.

1. Helping children to understand what forced sexual touch is.
2. Changing their attitude so that they know sexual abuse is not their fault.
3. Showing them that they have the right to tell someone until they are believed.
4. Being positive about the right kinds of touching.[3]

The program can be used in either a school or church setting.

The story traces the discoveries of "Bub"—an alien visitor— as she learns about good touch and bad touch. It is a delightful child's story that makes its point in a nonthreatening fashion.

The second resource is the Child Assault Prevention program (CAP) that was developed in Columbus, Ohio, several years ago. Its purpose is to empower children and to prevent them from being victims of assault by educating them, their parents, teachers, and others in the community.

CAP often is done in schools and led by specially trained persons. It has three components to it: a parent workshop, teacher/staff inservice, and a children's workshop.

One of the role plays in the children's session teaches that children can protect themselves from sexual abuse, even from someone they know and trust. When Uncle Harry strokes his niece and forces her to give him a kiss, he tells her to keep it a secret. The primary facilitator then discusses touching by observing that most of the time when people touch us it's a good touch. But sometimes someone might touch us (like Uncle Harry) in a way that doesn't make us feel safe. Kisses, hugs, and touches need to be mutual, not forced.

After the workshop, leaders remain behind for thirty minutes or so for consultation with any students who are confused or frightened.

Information on these and other materials is available through

The National Committee for Prevention
   of Child Abuse
332 South Michigan Avenue
Suite 1250
Chicago, Illinois 60604-4357
Phone (312) 663-3520

When churches decide to support the efforts of community
agencies, like the school, in preparing children to deal with sexual molestation, then the giant is coming alive.

For Worship

In the life of the church, nothing rivals worship as a means
of focusing public attention on a topic. The congregation that
cares about the evil of child sexual abuse also dares to lift it up
as a theme in worship. The risk is obvious because some people will think that molestation is an inappropriate subject for
worship. Opponents will usually let you know their views
without your having to ask. The greater risk for children,
offenders, and families is to remain silent.

April has traditionally been designated as Child Abuse Prevention Month by the National Committee for the Prevention
of Child Abuse. They in turn have prepared a resource packet
for religious leaders to use on child abuse prevention. It is entitled "For the Love of Children," and includes suggested activities for observing Prevention Month or Prevention Sunday.

The following is a sampling of the worship suggestions to be
found within the packet.

* * *

Call to Worship   Mark 10:13-16
People were bringing little children to Jesus to have him
touch them, but the disciples rebuked them. When Jesus saw
this, he was indignant. He said to them, "Let the little children
come to me, and do not hinder them, for the kingdom of God
belongs to such as these. I tell you the truth, anyone who will
not receive the kingdom of God like a little child will never

enter it." And he took the children in his arms, put his hands on them and blessed them.

Prayer of Confession

Almighty God, who taught us to serve one another as you have served us through your Son Jesus Christ, we confess that weariness keeps us from responding to the needs of others. Fear keeps us from loving the unlovely who cry for lack of compassion. Desire for the pretty and tranquil keeps us from seeking your redeeming beauty and peace that lie beyond the world's ugliness and tragedy. Forgive our weariness, our fear, and our complacency. Inspire us to face the cross of human suffering so that we may live as your true sons and daughters. Through Christ our Lord, amen.

Litany of Intercession

Leader: For families who are facing the loss of jobs or the pain and grief of divorce or death . . .
Response: Grant them comfort, O Lord.
Leader: For children and parents who live in conflict and misunderstanding . . .
Response: Grant them your peace, O Lord.
Leader: For single parents who experience the burden of raising children alone . . .
Response: Grant them courage and love, O Lord.
Leader: For infants and children who are abused by their parents and others who love them . . .
Response: Grant them healing and forgiveness, O Lord.
Leader: For peaceful resolve of all of our family conflicts . . .
Response: Grant us hope, O Lord.

Scripture Passages

Romans 12:21	Romans 7:15	Jeremiah 8:21-22
Luke 6:35-38	Matthew 9:9-13	1 John 4:19-21

* * *

These texts do not deal explicitly with child sexual abuse.

Indeed, except for Leviticus 18:6ff the Bible never deals directly with the topic. However, the previous passages do speak of justice, healing, forgiveness, and love, any one of which can be adapted for homiletic use.

The next chapter reprints a sermon that one minister delivered on the subject of child sexual abuse.

I am confident that the sleeping giant slowly is becoming alert and aware. In part this is true because the child sexual abuse story is being told by mothers like Joan. Let's hear the conclusion of her ordeal.

"In retrospect . . . let the growing and caring church demonstrate that there is hope for everyone whose lives are touched by this secret pain."[4]

9

Using the Sermon to Educate

Of all the ways of alerting congregations to the circumstances of child sexual abuse, the sermon reaches the largest audience and thereby creates the largest risk.

But some clergypersons are taking the risk.

Reverend Donald Allen is one who did so. Through his pastoral ministry at the Grandview Baptist Church in Kansas City, Kansas, Don became newly aware of the extent of the problem of child abuse. His sermon, abridged to include only the section that dealt with incest, follows.

* * *

Is It Fair?

Text: Numbers 14:18

"All I've ever known since I was a child is sex. As long as I can remember I was sexually exploited." These were the words of a desperate woman in her late twenties when she finally went to a counselor for help. She continued, "First it was my brothers and their friends, then my father . . . I hate all men!"

Incest takes an incalculable emotional toll and does almost irreparable damage to the lives of persons, keeping them from a healthy heterosexual relationship. This is especially true when a father or stepfather relates sexually to a daughter. The same is true when a mother sleeps with a son and sexual contact is made. In a mental institution a young man told his doctor that he frequently slept with and had sex with his mother. This might seem repulsive to us, but it happens. Incest is a common problem with which counselors are required to work.

Is it fair that children should be molested by unthinking, insensitive, and sexually starved parents or stepparents? The answer seems obvious. Of course it isn't! Numbers 14:18 declares

> The Lord is slow to anger, and abounding in steadfast love, forgiving iniquity and transgression, but he will by no means clear the guilty, visiting the iniquity of fathers upon children, upon the third and upon the fourth generation.

Incest influences not only one generation of children but also future generations as well. An important theological question presses upon us: Is it fair that the sins of the parents influence children in the generations to come? Again we must say that it is not fair to the children! The Scriptures never tell us that it is fair, yet it happens.

Parents are given a sacred responsibility to raise and influence their children in the ways of decency and righteousness. Parents are responsible for this. They are given precious power to mold their descendants in the ways of God. Sexual perversion can destroy the sacred trust endowed by our Creator to raise children who are healthy, happy, and capable of passing on this sacred trust with dignity and grace to their children.

Incest is a tragedy. Unfortunately it most often goes undetected. It remains a family secret because the offending parent intimidates the victim or in other emotional ways controls this demonic secret. Incestuous parents or other family members generally know the incestuous act is unlawful and socially reprehensible. Parents can be prosecuted for sexually abusing their children. One of the saddest persons I've ever known was a father who had related sexually with a daughter for a number of years. This daughter began to share her feelings with a young man, and the father became irate. Out of this conflict situation the behavior of the father came to the attention of civil authorities. Legal proceedings were swift and the man was on his way to prison. Never have I seen a more dejected, fearful, and pathetic person. For the sexual offender prison is probably the worst possible alternative in terms of rehabilitation and long-term help.

What happened to his daughter? I don't know for sure, but if she grew up like most victims she has had an unhappy life. What often happens is that children grow up with a terrible self-image. They often feel sad, dirty, sinful, and angry. They bury the angry feelings toward incestuous parents and live with depression for most of their adult lives. For the sexually molested child, healthy sexual gratification is very difficult, and such victims in turn can become incestuous. The sins of one generation become the sins of future generations.

What can be done about incest? The Bible relates stories of incest without giving much specific direction. An example of this is Lot and his two daughters in Genesis chapter 19. When Lot was drunk his daughters went in to him and each became pregnant by him. Since his daughters plotted it all, in a sense, the drunken father never knew what happened until later. As it often does in such situations of sexual abuse, the Bible offers no corrective or moral judgment about the activity.

Even today, an intoxicated father can lower his guard against inappropriate sexual activity and then excuse himself for his behavior because he didn't know what he was doing. The same is true for a mother. Parents need to be very careful about the use of intoxicating beverages and other mind-altering drugs, especially if there is temptation for incest.

However, there are parents who take a self-righteous stand against the use of drugs whose lives are sexually starved and unfulfilled. Sometimes such persons do understand their darker nature, keep it under control, and direct their energies into creative activity. If so, they are helped immensely if they have a trusted friend and counselor, such as their pastor, to help with this process.

Beyond increasing our awareness of incest, what can we do?

There is a great need to count on God's power and presence in every relationship. When we possess a positive, healthy view of sexuality, we are more apt to be led by God to real intimacy, healthy responsibilities, and gratification of our basic desires with which God has blessed us. Our outlook needs to be to trust God and keep on learning.

Meanwhile, for those who do violate the sacredness of God's trust, it must be remembered and taught that "The Lord is slow to anger and abounding in steadfast love, forgiving iniquity and transgressions." Forgiveness awaits all who are repentant about their betrayal of God's trust. May our persistent prayer be "God, open our eyes to see the tragedy of incest, and help us to never violate your trust."

Incest is unfair to the present generation and the children of the third and fourth generations.

*　*　*

Don Allen's timely message, growing out of his own knowledge of incestuous situations in his community, created a new awareness among God's people. It's safe to guess that no one slept during the sermon that day. The giant was awakened. Some three years after preaching that sermon, Don Allen is pastoring the same congregation and doing it with effectiveness.

The message for other concerned and courageous pastors is clear. Go, and do likewise!

Appendix

Resources

As an aid to the reader, I have marked each resource with an "audience level indicator." I also have included my judgment regarding the overall quality and value of each resource. By doing this I hope the reader will be spared the problem of trying to choose an appropriate resource from among many resources, all of which seem equally good.

The audience level indicator chart reads as follows:

C—Children (elementary grades)
ET—Early teens (junior high)
LT—Late teens (senior high)
P—Parents
PR—Professionals (in the field of child sexual abuse)
A—Adults and the general public

A four-star system to designate the quality and value of each item will be used. Four stars (****) means excellent; three stars (***) means good; two stars (**) means below average; one star (*) means not recommended.

Books

Adams, Caren, and Fay, Jennifer, *No More Secrets*. San Luis

Obispo, Calif.: Impact Publishers Inc., 1981, 90 pages.

This is a book designed to help parents talk to their children about sexual assault in the hope that children might be prepared to recognize and avoid becoming victims. It is practical and utilizes case histories and parental quotes to drive home its point that it is always right to talk about abuse and to report it to a trusted adult.

Audience level: P, A   Rating: ***

Butler, Sandra, *Conspiracy of Silence: The Trauma of Incest*. San Francisco: Volcano Press Inc., 1978, 206 pages.

This thoroughly researched and well-documented book explodes the misleading myth that incest is predominately a lower-class problem. It further reveals the disastrous effects of incest on the emotional and interpersonal development of children. Volcano Press is located at 330 Ellis Street, San Francisco, CA 94102.

Audience level: P, A, PR   Rating: ***

Daugherty, Lynn B., *Why Me?* (Help for Victims of Child Sexual Abuse). Racine: Mother Courage Press, 1984, 109 pages.

This book was written to help victims of child sexual abuse—even if the victims are now adults. It also was written for counselors who want to understand and help these victims. It contains stories of seventeen victims, illustrating a wide variety of sexual abuse situations. It teaches the victim that it is not his or her fault. Mother Courage Press is located at 1533 Illinois Street, Racine, WI 53405.

Audience level: ET, LT, A   Rating: ***

Finkelhor, David, *Child Sexual Abuse: New Theory and Research*. New York: The Free Press, 1984.

David Finkelhor, one of the nation's foremost authorities on sexual abuse, provides theoretical and research perspectives on abuse, including the nature of abuse, its dynamics, the larger social forces shaping public opinion, and professional attitudes. This is a necessary volume but it will not appeal to most church audiences.

Audience level: PR   Rating: ***

Fortune, Marie, *Sexual Abuse Prevention: A Study for Teenagers*. New York: United Church Press, 1984.

This is a five-session course of study for 12 to 18 year olds that has been field tested and found to be successful for adolescents in schools and youth groups—both rural and urban. It provides information about sexual abuse, distinguishing appropriate, healthy sexual contact from inappropriate, abusive contact. It offers ways of self-protection as well as community resources to help victims. The study deals with rape prevention and other sexual abuse.

Audience level: ET, LT, P   Rating: ***

Fortune, Marie, *Sexual Violence: The Unmentionable Sin*. New York: The Pilgrim Press, 1983, 237 pages.

This is must reading for religious leaders. It is well written by the foremost clergy authority in the field. An ethical and pastoral perspective is provided, including a survey of the few pertinent biblical passages on the subject. The last chapter calls upon the church to take responsible action, and it offers suggested strategies for church involvement.

Audience level: P, A, PR   Rating: ****

Gordon, Sol and Judith, *A Better Safe Than Sorry Book*. Fayetteville, New York: Ed U Press, 1984.

These well-known sex educators have written an excellent guide to help parents talk to their children (ages three to nine) about sexual abuse prevention. It is designed to be read together and teaches children how to say no in confusing situations. Illustrations are friendly depictions of normal children. A special section for parents gives general information about sexual abuse and suggests further reading.

Audience level: C, P   Rating: ****

Herman, Judith Lewis, *Father-Daughter Incest*. Cambridge, Mass.: Harvard University Press, 1981.

Through an intensive clinical study of forty incest victims and numerous interviews with mental health and other professionals, the author develops a composite picture of the incestuous family. It is written from a feminist perspective, with a

final chapter on preventing abuse in the family.
    Audience level: PR, A   Rating ***

Hill, Eleanore, *The Family Secret*. Santa Barbara, Calif.:
    Capra Press, 1985, 280 pages.
    In this true story the author examines with courage, candor,
and compassion the family dynamics of child sexual abuse.
This book reads like a novel, but is actually the true experience
of one woman as she deals with child sexual abuse. It is well
written. Capra Press is located at Box 2068, Santa Barbara, CA
93120.
    Audience level: P, A, PR   Rating: ***

Hyde, Margaret, *Sexual Abuse: Let's Talk About It*. Phila-
    delphia: The Westminster Press, 1984, 90 pages.
    Here is information on protection, prevention, and treat-
ment in the area of child sexual abuse. Through many case
histories, this volume shows that even young children can
learn to avoid inappropriate sexual touching and to realize they
are not to blame for what happens. An extensive state-by-state
listing of child sexual abuse treatment centers is a unique fea-
ture of this book.
    Audience level: A, P   Rating: ***

Mackey, Gene, and Swan, Helen, *Dear Elizabeth*. Leawood,
    Kansas: Children's Institute of Kansas City, 1983, 92 pages.
    Dear Elizabeth is a fictional account of one teenager's efforts
to deal with sexual abuse. Brenda is molested by her father,
and in her diary she describes the guilt, depression, and fear
that she experiences. She talks of wanting to die and of feeling
responsible for the breakup of her family. Her progress is
traced through both individual and group therapy, and gradually, as healing comes, she becomes a survivor rather than a
victim. This is an excellent book for understanding the trauma
of incest.
    Audience level: ET, LT, P, A   Rating: ****

Sweet, Phyllis E., *Something Happened to Me*. Racine:
    Mother Courage Press, 1981, 36 pages.

Professionals and others working with children who have been sexually abused will find this to be a useful tool. It is to be read by an adult to the child in the hope that the child will be encouraged to talk about his or her own experiences rather than keeping sexual abuse a secret and perhaps feeling guilty. A minimum story line and use of simple illustrations makes this an excellent educational piece for children.

Audience level: C, PR, P   Rating: ***

Films

Incest: The Victim Nobody Believes, 20 minutes, MTI Teleprograms, 3710 Commercial Avenue, Northbrook, IL 60062.

Three young women informally discuss their experiences of incestuous relationships with their fathers. The guilt, fear, confusion, depression, and shame are powerfully evident. One says, "I walked around for years thinking there was something wrong with *me*." Another talks of suicide. The fathers are depicted as being gentle and nurturing even when involved in sexual acts with their daughters. This film is unrivaled in showing the emotional pain of victims.

Audience level: ET, LT, P, A, PR   Rating: ****

The Hidden Shame, 19 minutes, MTI Teleprograms.

This is the true story (as shown originally on ABC's "20/20") of two adult sisters who prosecuted their abusing father. Their action was a divisive one within the family. The film deals some with therapy for offenders. In one memorable scene an offender talks about the causes for his behavior, including a "strict mother." We see the weaknesses and insecurities of offenders in a candid fashion.

Audience level: LT, A, P   Rating: ***

Who Do You Tell? 10 minutes, MTI Teleprograms.

Using a combination of animation and live footage of children talking, the film shows responses to scary situations by children faced with sexual abuse. Addressed to children age seven to twelve, the film describes the support a child has both in the family and in the community when sexual abuse is present. However, the presentation is too simplistic to be of much value.

Audience level: C, A   Rating: *

Some Secrets Should Be Told, 12 minutes, MTI Teleprograms, 1982 (Also on videocassette).

Two puppets talk about an uncle's improper touching of a little girl named Elizabeth. It deals with proper touching as well and stresses that secrets should always be told to a trusted adult. It is a cute presentation geared to younger children, but other films are better.

Audience level: C   Rating: **

Incest: Hidden Crime, 20 minutes, The Media Guild, Box 881, 118 South Acacia Avenue, Solana Beach, CA 92075.

This is an actual case history of an incestuous father-daughter relationship. Excellent insights are given to pinpoint the causes of the father's behavior: a rejecting, nonresponsive wife, submissive daughter, and father with absolute authority in the home. Treatment for offenders is shown. In one scene the therapist says, "Then father is the only one out of role. Because if he has a rejecting wife and a submissive child, he still has the choice whether to sexualize the situation or not." A very helpful film.

Audience level: A, PR, P   Rating: ****

Bubbylonian Encounter, 27 minutes, Kansas Committee for the Prevention of Child Abuse, 435 S. Kansas Avenue, Second Floor, Topeka, KS 66603.

Adapted from a play of the same name, this film is lively, sensitive, and humorous. It brings a space visitor named Bub to earth. Bub has to learn about the many dimensions of touching. She learns the positive rewards of touching as well as its perils. Throughout the film Bub is a role model for children in her lack of knowledge about touching and her assertive manner of dealing with forced sexual touching.

Audience level: C, ET, P, A, PR   Rating: ****

Don't Get Stuck There, 14 minutes, Communication and Public Service, Boys Town Center, Boys Town, NE 68010.

This film for teenagers has former victims of sexual abuse describing the physical, emotional, and sexual abuse that they suffered at the hands of their parents. Before seeking professional help, each tried drugs, alcohol, or suicide. This film does not deal exclusively with sexual abuse and is therefore less valuable than others.

Audience level: LT, P, A, PR   Rating: **

The Touching Problem, 18 minutes, MTI Teleprograms (Also on videocassette).

Originally produced for television this film deals with one child's experience with the unwelcome touch of an uncle. While some good information is included, the resource is preachy, lacks integration of purpose, and seems too sensationalistic at points.

Audience level: P, A   Rating: **

Videocassettes

Better Safe Than Sorry II, 14 minutes, Filmfair Communications, Box 1728, 10900 Ventura Blvd., Studio City, CA 91604 (Also on film).

This video is designed to help children avoid situations of potential sexual abuse and to teach them what to do if such a situation arises. A group of children play "let's pretend" with the narrator. They decide how they would respond under certain potential circumstances. Through repetition three rules are driven home: Say no, Get away, Tell someone. This is an outstanding resource for use in the elementary grades.

Audience level: C, P, PR   Rating: ****

No More Secrets, 13 minutes, O.D.N. Productions, 74 Varick Street, New York, NY 10013 (Also on film).

Four 11-year-old friends confide in one another about family members who touch and sexually abuse them. The strong point of this video is that it stresses the importance of disclosing sexual abuse, and shows how to say no to inappropriate behavior. However, some animated sequences are potentially scary, and the video lacks a clear and repeated message.

Audience level: C, P, PR   Rating: **

Strong Kids—Safe Kids, 1984, 42 minutes (Available at most video stores).

Henry Winkler (The Fonz) stars in this video, and he, along with experts like Sol Gordon and Kee MacFarlane, teach parents and children basic skills for preventing sexual abuse. This resource is entertaining as well as educational and is designed to be watched by parents and their children (ages 3 to 12) together.

Audience level: C, ET, P, A   Rating: ***

Touch, 32 minutes, MTI Teleprograms (Also on film).

Touch is an outstanding resource for dealing with all aspects of touching, from nurturing to exploitive, including information about sexual touching. To its credit it depicts good touching as well as bad touching. The video was produced by Minnesota's well-known Illusion Theater and moderated by Lindsay Wagner.

Audience level: C, ET, LT, P, A, PR   Rating: ****

An Ounce of Prevention, 1983, 18 minutes, Agency for Instructional Technology, Box A, Bloomington, IN 47402.

Actually, this resource is three videos for three different age groups: 4–8, 9–11, and 12–14. Each of the videos concerns a racially mixed group of children spelling out a very clear set of rules when confronted with sexual abuse. Rules like Say no, Get away, and Tell someone are included along with some valuable additions: Your body belongs to you, Trust your feelings, and Walk assertively. These are well-made videos with appropriate age-level learning methods. Instruction manuals are included.

Audience level: C, ET, P, A   Rating: ****

Programs and Curricula

Fortune, Marie, "Family Violence: A Workshop Manual for

Clergy and Other Service Providers," 1980, National Clearinghouse, Rockville, Maryland.

This program was prepared particularly to train religious leaders in dealing with family violence. It has some useful sessions on child sexual abuse, but covers the whole range of abuse as well. The manual is quite detailed in setting forth the goals, objectives, strategies, exercises, and evaluations of a training event. Marie Fortune is an ordained minister in the United Church of Christ.

Audience level: P, PR, A   Rating: ***

Kent, Cordelia Anderson, "Child Sexual Abuse Prevention Project: An Educational Program for Children," 1979, Hennipin County Attorney's Office, C-2100 Goverment Center, Minneapolis, MN 55487.

The foundation of this curriculum is the "touch continuum," which explores the difference between touch that is nurturing versus touch that is damaging. This resource teaches how to implement a child sexual abuse program at K–12 levels with an emphasis on elementary grades.

Audience level: PR, elementary and secondary teachers   Rating: ***

Olson, Marlys, "Personal Safety: Curriculum for the Prevention of Child Sexual Abuse," Council on Child Abuse, Box 1357, Tacoma, WA 98401.

Produced in 1982, this comprehensive curriculum includes bibliographical information and complete lesson plans for Headstart, K–2, 3–4, 5–6, Junior High, and Senior High. A teacher's manual is included. Four topics are covered at each level: personal safety, touching, assertiveness techniques, and support systems.

Audience level: C, ET, LT, PR   Rating: ***

Child Assault Prevention Project, Women Against Rape, Box 02084, Columbus, Ohio 43202.

This program for children in elementary school (ages 5–12) emphasizes the child's right to be safe, strong, and free. It also offers a workshop for parents. The children's workshop, lasting one hour, features four role plays that help children learn to deal with various forms of abuse, including sexual abuse.

Audience level: P, PR, C   Rating: ***

The Happy Bear Project, Kansas Committee for the Prevention of Child Abuse, 435 S. Kansas Avenue, Second Floor, Topeka, Kansas 66603.

This program is for preschoolers and teaches them about touch and how to recognize and protect themselves from sexual assault. It is a live presentation, with audience participation, featuring a lovable bear character named Happy Bear and a mental health professional. An instructor's manual, videotape, and teacher training are all available. This project has been used in at least 22 states and is widely acclaimed.

Audience level: C, P, PR   Rating: ****

One final, general resource listing may be helpful: Child Sexual Abuse Prevention Resources, published in 1985 by the National Committee for the Prevention of Child Abuse, 332 S. Michigan Avenue, Suite 1250, Chicago, Illinois 60604-4357, (312) 663-3520. In this most comprehensive guide, over 180 books, films, videos, programs, curricula, and plays are listed. We strongly urge churches to send for this resource.

 Notes

Chapter 4

[1]Fortune, Marie, *Sexual Violence: The Unmentionable Sin.* New York: The Pilgrim Press/United Church Press, 1983.

Chapter 5

[1]Bok, Sissela, "The Limits of Confidentiality," The Hastings Center Report, February 1983, pp. 24–25.
[2]Fortune, Marie, "Confidentiality and Mandatory Reporting: A Clergy Dilemma?" Source unknown.
[3]*Ibid.*
[4]Kansas Child Abuse and Neglect Reporting Act, K.S.A. 38-717.
[5]Kansas Child Abuse and Neglect Reporting Act, K.S.A. 38-722.
[6]Kansas Child Abuse and Neglect Reporting Act, K.S.A. 38-717.
[7]Dawson, Seth

Chapter 7

[1]Peters, David B. *The Betrayal of Innocence*, p. 120.
[2]*Ibid.*, p. 124.
[3]Fortune, *Sexual Violence*, pp. 209–210.
[4]Wiggen, Cooper, "The Christian Minister," May 1987, p. 24.
[5]Wiggen, "The Christian Minister," May 1987, p. 26.

Chapter 8

[1]This story appeared in "Watchword," vol. II, no. 2, June/July 1987. "Watchword" is a newsletter produced by the American Baptist Churches' Women in Ministry Program. Mary Mild is the editor.
[2]From a 1979 CBS news production film entitled "Incest," in *March* magazine.
[3]Swan, Helen, "Bubbylonian Encounter" brochure.
[4]"Watchword."

LINCOLN CHRISTIAN COLLEGE AND SEMINARY